HOW?D THEY DO THAT?

in ...

PRE-COLUMBIAN AMERICA

Mitchell Lane
PUBLISHERS

P.O. Box 196
Hockessin, Delaware 19707

HOW?D THEY
DO THAT?

in...

PRE-COLUMBIAN
AMERICA

MARYLOU MORANO KJELLE

Mitchell Lane

PUBLISHERS

Printing   1   2   3   4   5   6   7   8   9

Library of Congress Cataloging-in-Publication Data
Kjelle, Marylou Morano.
  How'd they do that in pre-Columbian America / by Marylou Morano Kjelle.
       p. cm.–(How'd they do that)
  Includes bibliographical references and index.
  ISBN 978-1-58415-826-4 (library bound)
  1. Indians of North America—History—Juvenile literature. 2. Indians of North America—Social life and customs—Juvenile literature. 3. North America—Civilization, Ancient. I. Title.
  E77.4.K565 2010
  970.004'97–dc22

                                                                2009027341

AUTHOR'S NOTE: Although the term "pre-Columbian civilizations" includes those peoples who lived in North, Central, and South America before Christopher Columbus arrived in 1492 and for a period of time thereafter, this book focuses on the pre-Columbian peoples of North America. The lifestyles of the Aztecs and Mayas of Central America are the subject of *How'd They Do That in the Aztec Empire* and *How'd They Do That in the Mayan Civilization*.

PUBLISHER'S NOTE: This story is based on the author's extensive research, which she believes to be accurate. Documentation of his research is on page 59.

The internet sites referenced herein were active as of the publication date. Due to the fleeting nature of some web sites, we cannot guarantee they will all be active when you are reading this book.

                                                                PLB

CONTENTS

Twelve-year old Unami sprang from his blanket-bed the minute he saw the sun's pink haze light up the sky. He had been too excited to sleep, and had spent the entire night thinking about what would happen in the morning. Today was the day of his Hunting Skills Test, a test Unami, like all young boys of the Iroquois tribe, needed to pass if he wanted to be considered a hunter and warrior.

There was another reason Unami wanted to pass the Hunting Skills Test. Passing would honor his teachers. According to the traditions of his tribe, a young boy was taught hunting and warrior skills by his mother's brothers. The clan elders had chosen Unami's uncles Tamarind and Yahgan to be his teachers. Unami's father, Hurit, was teaching his cousin, Kimi.

Tamarind and Yahgan had been teaching Unami since the Hard Times Moon of Biting Winds and Long Nights*. One of Unami's first tests had been the Personal Endurance Test. For this test, he'd had to

*The month of January

swim in an ice-covered lake. First, he had to break the ice, then stay in the water until his uncles said he could come out. When at last he was called from the water, he was wrapped in animal furs and brought back to the longhouse to warm up near the cooking fire.

The Personal Endurance Test had been difficult, but Unami had pleased his uncles. Before he broke the ice and jumped into the water, he had prayed to one of his clan's totems, the Frog, whose animal spirit represented a connection with water. Unami felt the Frog's spirit enter and strengthen him as he endured the test.

Another part of Unami's education had been learning to hunt animals for food. Unami had spent many days and nights in the forest, trapping and hunting with his uncles. Today he would be tested on those skills. He would enter the forest with just his spear and spear-thrower, or atlatl, and he would not be allowed to return to the village until he had caught an animal.

Corn cakes were pancakes made with cornmeal. Some pre-Columbian people called corn a "gift of the Gods."

Before he could leave for the forest, however, Unami had to eat his morning meal. He moved toward the cooking fire where his mother, Wikimak, was preparing flat cakes made from cornmeal. Wikimak was proud of her son and of what he would be challenged to do that day. She urged him to take an extra corn cake and more of the tea she had brewed from the bark of a nearby tree. It sometimes took a young man more than one day to return from the forest with his prey, and he could neither eat nor drink until he returned.

"It may be a while until you again take nourishment," Wikimak said, worried. "Eat enough to carry your strength with you."

"Don't worry, mother. I will bring honor to our clan," said Unami.

"I wish I could bring honor to our clan by hunting," said Unami's younger sister, Suki. "I get so tired of weaving baskets and picking vegetables."

Unami smiled at Suki. He had to agree. The boys' training did seem more exciting than the training the girls received in maintaining a home.

As soon as Unami finished his morning meal, he was on his way. With a nod to his mother and the rest of his clan, he followed Tamarind and Yahgan to the edge of the forest. There the group met the tribe's holy man, Nuttah, who performed a special dance to the Great Spirit for Unami's success. Nuttah lit a ceremonial pipe and blew tobacco smoke on Unami to purify him. Then Yahgan handed Unami a large shell filled with black soot from a cooled fire.

"Smear this on your face," Yahgan commanded.

Unami did as he was told. His blackened face was a sign to other hunters that he might meet in the forest. It said that Unami was being tested and that he was not to be given help. Yahgan gave Unami his atlatl and his spears. Then his uncles turned back to the village, and Unami headed into the forest.

Pre-Columbian people prayed to different gods for different needs. A ceremony before a hunt always asked the blessing of enough prey to feed the clan.

As he made his way through the trees, Unami prayed to his totems. He asked the Ram for strength, the Salmon for determination, and the Dog for protection.

For a long time, Unami quietly roamed the forest. Through a clearing in the trees, he could see the sun was directly overhead. This told him that it was midday, but he neither heard nor saw an animal. He was thirsty, and his stomach was rumbling from hunger. Sweat streaked down his sooty face. Still he kept walking and praying, all the while listening for the sound of the animal that his totems would send him.

The sun was low in the sky when he heard a rustling sound and saw a rabbit standing under a bush. Softly Unami spoke to his prey. He apologized for what he was about to do and asked the rabbit for forgiveness. He told the rabbit that it was an honored animal to be chosen by the totems to be slain in a Hunting Skills Test. Unami then thanked the rabbit for its sacrifice.

It was dark when Unami made his way back to his village, holding the dead rabbit in his hand. He was quickly brought to his longhouse, where his face was washed and he was given food and drink. Later that evening there would be a celebration for him. Members of his clan would eat, drink, and dance in his honor. But right now, all Unami wanted to do was sit by the fire and rest. It had been a long day, and he had been successful. He had passed his test.

Who Were the Pre-Columbian Americans?

Christopher Columbus was searching for a shorter way to sail from Europe to Asia when he discovered a "New World" in 1492. It might have been new to Columbus, but the world he discovered was really quite ancient. In fact, prehistoric people known as Paleo-Americans had been living in the pre-Columbian ("before Columbus") Americas for thousands of years.

Who were these ancient people and where did they come from? Questions like these are difficult to answer because no one was recording history back then. All sorts of theories arise when there is no record of an important event, but here's what most anthropologists—the scientists who study ancient people—think happened.

Paleo-Americans sheltered by a cave

Between 2 million and 10,000 years ago, when much of the world was covered by ice, the continents of Asia and North America were connected by a mass of dry, ice-free land called the Bering Land Bridge. Probably about 13,000 years ago, a small group of nomadic *Homo sapiens* walked east across the Bering Land Bridge, from Siberia in Asia to Alaska in North America.[1] Not all of these early nomadic peoples stayed in one place. They followed rivers and crossed plains to different parts of the Americas. They settled in forests, mountains, deserts, and prairies, and near rivers, streams, and oceans. They survived by hunting, gathering wild foods, fishing, and developing agriculture. Gradually, the Paleo-Americans organized into specialized cultures or traditions that reflected their way of life.

How do anthropologists know about the daily lives of pre-Columbian Americans? They look at geological evidence, such as dried-up lakes, to see what the environment used to be like. They study tools, fossils, pieces of pottery and other artifacts found in caves. They also look at the growth and evolution of plants such as corn to try to place early Americans in a particular place at a particular time. Graves and burial sites can also tell us a lot about what it was like to be alive in pre-Columbian times.

The fossilized skeleton of a mastodon. These elephant-like mammals were nearly 10 feet (3 meters) tall at the shoulders.

HOW DID THEY GET THEIR FOOD?

Chapter 1

Anthropologists believe that the first humans to cross the Bering Land Bridge into America were probably hunters looking for food. They hunted the reindeer, buffalo (bison), wild horses, camels, musk oxen, and black bears that freely roamed the North American forests and plains in pre-Columbian times. Three other prehistoric creatures—now all extinct—were also hunted for food. They were the giant sloth (called *Megatherium*) and two large elephant-like mammals, the mastodon and the mammoth. The mammoth weighed several tons and had tusks that were eight to sixteen feet long. One of them provided enough food for several families for weeks.

It took centuries for the bow and arrow to be developed, and guns weren't used in North America until the Europeans brought them. How did pre-Columbian people hunt? One way was with a spear and an early hunting tool called an atlatl (OT-lah-tul). An atlatl was a piece of notched wood about eighteen inches long into which the spear was placed. A spear hurled from an atlatl would travel faster and farther than a spear thrown by hand. Spear points were four or five inches long and made from flint—a type of hard stone. How did pre-Columbians sharpen them? By flint knapping—scraping the flint against another stone. As pieces of the flint flaked off during the scraping, a sharp point was formed. Once the spear point was sharpened, it was fitted into a wooden shaft. Animal sinew or hide was wrapped around both the point and shaft to keep them together. These spear points have been found in Clovis, New Mexico. For this reason, they are known as Clovis points.[1]

It took more than one hunter to take down a mastodon or mammoth, so pre-Columbians hunted in groups. They quietly stalked an animal, spearing it every chance they got. When the animal was so weak that it could no longer move, it was killed either by a final spear stab to the heart or by clubbing it to death. Smaller animals, such as rabbits, were killed by boomerangs or chased into net traps by screaming children. The nets were about as long as those used today to play tennis. They were made of vines, sinew, soft tree bark, or braided buffalo fur or horsehair. Some native peoples lured their prey by dressing

Pre-Columbian people made most of their tools and other objects by hand. Sharp tools were made of shells, wood, stone and the bones of animals.

The buffalo was one of the most important animals for the pre-Columbians. Not only did it provide meat, but its bones, skin, internal organs, hoofs, and other body parts were used to make everyday objects.

in skins and hides and mimicking mating calls. Wild birds such as turkeys and geese were killed with spears in their nests at night.

The pre-Columbian people of the plains hunted the buffalo not only for its meat, but also for its hide. They didn't spear the buffalo; they drove them off cliffs. Buffalo drives usually occurred in the late fall when the buffalo were good and fat from summer grazing. Tribe members, including the children, would chase the buffalo with fiery torches, dogs, and screams. Sometimes hunters set fire to grazing land. All of these activities frightened the buffalo and forced entire herds to stampede over a cliff and fall to their deaths. Because the Plains hunters could not control how many animals were killed, this method of hunting was often wasteful.

The Thule were often subjected to temperatures that fell below 0°F. They hunted walrus, whale, and seal, and used sleds to travel over the frozen landscape.

The Thule, the ancestors of the Eskimos, lived along the coast of the Arctic Ocean for at least four thousand years before Columbus arrived. These sea-mammal hunters hunted caribou in the summer, but their main sources of food during the winter were the bowhead whale, the walrus, and the seal. To hunt these animals, a group of ten Eskimos paddled out onto the water in an umiak, a light boat made of walrus hide stretched over a frame made of driftwood. Once they saw their prey, they harpooned it. The harpoon is a hunting tool similar to the spear, but with a barbed head.

By Day or By Night: How Did They Fish?
The early peoples who settled in what would become the northwest coast of the United States mostly fished for their food. They went out into the water in dugouts—canoes made from hollowed-out logs. How did they make a wooden canoe without power tools or electricity? They

cut down a tree with an ax made of stone, and then set the tree on fire. They used stones and shells to scrape the charred wood out of the tree's center, until the log had a flat bottom and straight sides.

Fish were caught in weirs, which were miniature fences built across streams. Unable to jump over the fence, the trapped fish were netted or stabbed with special fishing spears that had points made from antler or bone. Northwest coast fisherman liked to fish after dark when the fish were more plentiful. How did they do this? They placed torches in their canoes. Not only did the torches make it easier to see, but the light attracted the fish to the canoes. Salmon was the main food of the natives living in the Northwest, but halibut, cod, smelt, and herring were also important foods.

On the Move: How Did They Gather?

Whether they were fishers or hunters, pre-Columbian people supplemented their diets with what they could gather from their surroundings. They depended on nuts, berries, acorns, roots, seeds, and fruits to keep

Pre-Columbian people depended on fish for food in the warmer months. Even the young could help with fishing. Fish that could not be eaten right away was dried in the sun and saved for the future.

their bellies full. They stripped bark from the trees, then ate it raw or cooked, or ground it into flour to make bread. Would you eat a beetle or grasshopper if you were hungry? What about a snake or a lizard? When game was scarce and there was no other food to be had, pre-Columbian gatherers ate all of these things, as well as many creatures most modern Americans would never think of eating.

Gathering food wasn't always as easy as picking berries or collecting acorns. Some plants, such as the sotol or agave, had razor-sharp spikes. To get to the edible roots and bulbs, gatherers dug underneath the plant with a digging stick—a small tree limb sharpened to a point with a stone.

Food gathering was usually done by the women and children, who placed what they found in baskets they made themselves. The summer and fall were the best seasons for foraging. Whatever they couldn't eat was dried in the sun and placed in pottery jars. Excess food was stored for later use in underground pits or storage areas in their homes.

People crushed dried, shelled acorns into meal. Then they leached the bitter tannin out of the meal. Acorns were convenient because they could be stored for years at a time without spoiling.

Pre-Columbians who depended heavily on gathering and foraging for their food were always on the move. Why didn't they stay in one place? After they had gathered all there was to eat for the season, they either had to move or starve.

The Lay of The Land: How Did They Farm?
Agriculture was developed around 500 to 900 CE—later than hunting, fishing, and gathering—and it first happened with maize in Central and South America. By this time the ancient wild horses that had greeted early nomads were extinct, and early farmers had to grow food without the help of animals. Between hunting expeditions, the men cleared and plowed the land. How did they do this without a backhoe or tractor? One way was to cut back as much vegetation as possible with primitive stone knives and then set it on fire. This method of clearing land is called slash and burn, and it made the fields rich in nutrients.[2] Crops grown on land cleared by the slash-and-burn method did well for a few growing seasons, and then the fields were left alone to recover.

A planting stick

How did they plant their seeds? With a planting stick. Like the digging stick used by the gatherers, a planting stick was a sturdy tree limb with one end sharpened to a point. The point was jabbed into the ground, and seeds were dropped into the holes it made. Another type of plant-ing stick they used had a rounded edge, like our present-day shovel. This made it useful for turning soil. What about storms that destroyed crops? The farm-ing peoples protected their crops by planting fields in many different locations, and by staggering their planting times throughout the grow-ing season.

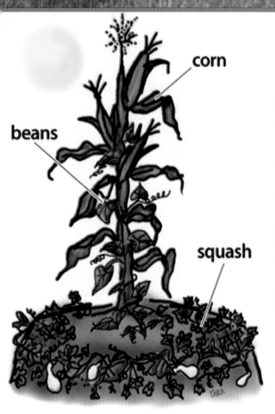

The Three Sisters

Crops were usually situated as close as possible to a source of water. The water was directed to the crops through channels constructed from stone. Once the crops were planted, the women and children took over the growing and harvesting.

Pre-Columbian Woodland natives of eastern North America grew corn, beans, and squash—a group called the Three Sisters. When the three were planted near each other, the vines of the squash and beans climbed the cornstalks. Pumpkins, melons, peppers, onions, chilies, and tobacco were also grown in small gardens. What did they use for fertilizer? Shells and chopped fish. How did they keep deer and crows from eating the crops? The older children climbed onto a platform built above the crops. They scared off deer and crows by throwing stones at them.[3]

Wild rice grew in shallow lakes and streams. Rice harvesting parties went out in canoes and pulled the grains from the rice plants. The grains fell into the bottom of the canoes. When the boats were filled with rice, the parties returned to shore. They carried the rice back to camp in baskets or pottery containers. Several canoe loads could be harvested in a single day.

How Did They Cook Their Food?

Most Pre-Columbian homes had a cooking fire in which they roasted, boiled, smoked, or baked their food. Meat and wild birds were roasted on a spit made by laying a stick across a cooking fire. Fish was usually smoked. Without refrigeration, extra meat and fish were cut into strips, dried on racks in the sun, and saved for future meals.

They also used the cooking fire to heat stones for cooking. They would drop red-hot rocks into a bowl or basket of water and other food, such as vegetables. The hot rocks brought the water to a boil and cooked the food.[4]

Pre-Columbians also used stones as metates (muh-TAH-tees), or grinders for seeds, corn, and acorns. What did they use as seasoning? Animal grease or maple sugar and syrup, which they made from the sap of maple trees. Honey was also used to sweeten food.

Men were the hunters in the pre-Columbian societies. They went into the forests to hunt the meat and brought it home for the women to cook.

Maize and
Cornmeal Mush

Maize, the cereal grain we call corn, had been grown in the Americas for thousands of years before Columbus arrived. Corn was an especially important food of the native farmers of the Southwest. They roasted it on the cob or dried the kernels in the sun. They used a metate—a two-stone grinder—to grind the dried kernels into cornmeal. The larger the stones of the metate, the coarser the cornmeal would be. Water was added to cornmeal to form a batter, which was shaped into little cakes or dumplings and baked. What did they use for ovens? They layered hot stones and leaves over a cooking fire and covered the layers with earth. The batter was spooned onto a hot rock. The hot leaves were put over the batter. In this manner the batter—in between hot rocks and hot leaves—baked into cakes.

Pre-Columbians also had their own version of "trail mix" for when they were on a hunting or fishing expedition. They mixed corn flour with dried fish or meat, then added a bit of animal fat or fish oil and a handful of berries or seeds.[5] This energetic protein- and fat-filled snack is known as pemmican.

Sometimes cornmeal batter was mixed in water to make a drink. Sometimes it was boiled and eaten as mush. The mush was most likely prepared by the women who accompanied the hunters or fishers on their trips. They boiled water in pitch-coated baskets, and stirred the mush with sticks. Everyone ate from the same pot by ladling the mush into their mouths using shells as spoons. Pre-Columbian people would have used any type of seed, nut, or berry that they had handy as a "topping" for the mush. The following recipe has been changed a little to allow for conveniences like the stove, but the cornmeal mush should look and taste the same as the snack eaten by pre-Columbian peoples hundreds of years ago.

Cornmeal Mush
(Serves 4)

Ask an adult to help you prepare this snack.
You will need:
a measuring cup
a large spoon for stirring
a small pot
oven mitt
serving bowls and spoons

Ingredients:
1¼ cups of water
1 8-oz. box of prepared corn muffin mix
¾ teaspoon of salt
a pat or two of butter or margarine, or some maple syrup
a handful of blueberries or other berries or nuts

1. **Ask an adult** to boil water on the stove.
2. Empty the package of corn muffin mix into a bowl.
3. Stir the salt into the mix.
4. When the water comes to a boil, **have the adult** carefully pour it into the muffin mix–salt mixture a little at a time, stirring as he or she pours. Stop pouring when there are no dry particles of mix left and the mush is smooth, like applesauce or pudding. It's okay if you don't use all the water.
5. Add the butter or margarine and, if you'd like, a little maple syrup.
6. Serve in bowls, then top each serving with the blueberries or nuts.

A First Nations totem pole outside a longhouse in British Columbia, Canada. The First Nations of Canada include the Abenaki, Cree, Ojibwa, Haida, Iroquois, and other groups.

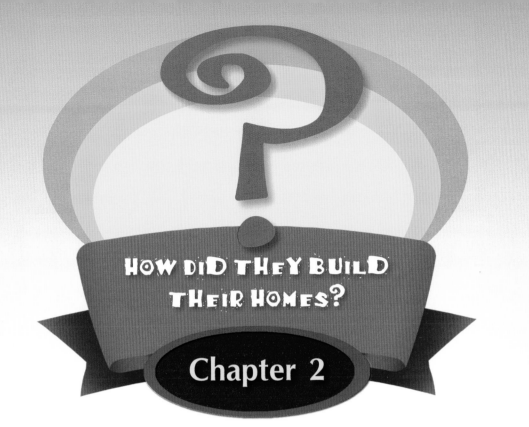

HOW DID THEY BUILD THEIR HOMES?

Chapter 2

Pre-Columbian housing varied according to where the people lived and how they acquired food. Crude camps, simple villages, and elaborate cities were all evident during pre-Columbian times. Early native peoples had a great respect for nature, and they constructed their homes mostly from natural resources. Family members with a common ancestor made up a clan, and often several clans lived together in one house. Each clan had its own symbol called a totem. Most pre-Columbian dwellings displayed the clan's totem pole either inside or outside the home.

Mobile Homes

Imagine being able to take your house apart and bring it with you wherever you go. That's what some pre-Columbian Americans did. The Haida were hunters and fishers who lived in the northwest section of North America. Their dwellings, which were rectangular plank houses, were made from the wood and bark of cedar trees. The walls of the home were roped together at the corners. When it was time to move to another camp, the entire house was taken apart and carried from one place to another. How did they do that? They carried them on their backs using a tumpline—a band that wrapped around their forehead and attached to the load packed on their shoulders.[1] Once they got to their new camp, they put their house back together again. Several families—about forty to sixty people—shared each Haida home. But it wasn't all "share and share alike." Each family had its own living quarters and cooked its own meals in the fire that burned continuously in the center of the house. The smoke from the fire escaped through a hole in the roof.

Woodland farmers lived in a round structure with a round or pointed roof called a wigwam. Making wigwams was women's work. They bent four saplings to make a frame, then used sinew to sew sheets of birch bark over it. To keep the bark from tearing, the women kept it wet as they sewed. They also overlapped the sheets, which helped keep out the wind and rain. They lined the inside with swamp grass to insulate the dwelling. Wigwams were used for sleeping, storage, and protection from the weather.

Wherever the buffalo roamed was where the Plains people made their home. Since they were constantly following the herds, they also needed homes that were easily transportable. Their mobile homes were tepees. The tepee looked something like a wigwam. It was a framework of poles arranged in a cone, but instead of birch bark, animal hides were fastened to the poles. A circle of stones held down the bottom of the

A wigwam

2

tepee. This type of dwelling could be as tall as 12 feet and need as many as 15 animal hides to completely cover it. Tepees were owned separately by men and women. The men of some tribes painted the outside of their tepee as a way to obtain special favors from the gods, such as favorable weather.[2] What did they use for paint? Red ocher, a pigment that comes from the iron that is found naturally in the earth. They also used natural plant dyes. Both tepees and wigwams had a fire pit in the center, which gave warmth and light and was used for cooking.[3] Tepees were transported from camp to camp with a travois—a sled-like contraption that was pulled by a dog.

A tepee

Pit Houses

The Hohokam were prehistoric farming peoples who migrated from Central America to Arizona around 300 BCE–500 CE. The Hohokam had several different styles of homes, but they often lived in small villages of pit houses—square or rectangular homes that were constructed several feet beneath the ground. A pit house was usually one room with raised areas for sleeping. The roof and walls were mud-covered platforms made from twigs, reeds, grass, and some of the earth that had been removed from the pit. The roof was supported by timbers. Why build a home partially underground? It had built-in climate control. The earth that surrounded the house kept it warm in winter and cool in summer.

Prehistoric Apartment Complexes

The Anasazi were basket makers who settled in what would become known as the Four Corners—the area where the borders of Arizona, New Mexico, Utah, and Colorado meet.[4] As these pre-Columbian people passed through many phases of development, they had many styles of housing. By around 1000 BCE, they were living in pueblos—towns or villages of cliff houses constructed of adobe and mud, and built into the side of caves. Like prehistoric apartment buildings, pueblos could rise as high as four stories. Some even had terraces, but the windows of the pueblo were small. Why? To keep out the heat of the desert.

Entering a cliff house was tricky. You had to climb down a ladder placed in a hole in the roof. Inside each house, ledges were used as

The Anasazi lived in cliff houses made of adobe and mud. Built as they were into the sides of mountains and caves, they resembled modern high-rise apartment buildings.

seats as well as to store shell ornaments, jewelry, clothing, weapons and tools. Food was stored in special pits dug into the cave floors. When they were no longer needed for food storage, these underground pits were used to bury the dead. A cliff house might have hundreds of rooms where dozens of family members lived together. What did they use for beds? Hide rugs or animal skins. Blankets were made by cutting animal fur into strips, twisting them around yucca fibers, and weaving them together. What was one good thing about living in a cliff house? Living so high up gave good protection from enemies and wild animals.

Longhouses

Woodland-dwelling natives such as the Iroquois lived in permanent villages deep within the forest. Their homes, structures made from saplings and bark, were called longhouses. A longhouse might be as long as 125 feet. It had a narrow hallway with several fire pits down

the center. A curtain made from animal skins served as a front door. Like other pre-Columbian peoples, several generations of many families lived together in one longhouse. Each family planted its own garden of corn, beans, squash, and tobacco, but all families shared the center fire pits for cooking. How did they separate each family's living area? With leather curtains. What did they use for furniture? Bunks built into the walls were used as chairs during the day. At night, covered with cornhusks and blankets made from skins and furs, the bunks became beds. The space under the bunk was used for storage. Higher shelves stored food and personal possessions. Longhouses were often arranged in a village of houses built around a central courtyard and protected by a fence. An image of the family living in the longhouse was painted over the door, letting everyone in the village know which family lived there.

Igloos

The Thule settled in the coldest regions of North America: Canada and Greenland. In the winter, when they were hunting sea mammals, these ancient people lived in igloos, round dwellings made from bricks of snow. How did they make the snow bricks? They cut them with knives sharpened on ice and stone. Inside the igloo were shelves which the Thule covered with fur and animal skins. These were used as beds. How did they keep the inside of the igloo warm? They used lamps that burned blubber. Sealskin draped around the igloo's walls helped keep it dry. During their summer hunting breaks away from the water, the Eskimos lived in tents made from animal hides.

Interior of an igloo

FYInfo

Totem Poles: Prehistoric History Books

Totems were sacred objects, usually animals that a clan chose to be its symbols. An animal was chosen to be a totem because of its special traits and religious importance. Birds, bears, and deer were popular Pre-Columbian totems. A deer represented gentleness and kindness, while a bear represented power. The buffalo stood for good fortune, and fish represented the life force that came from water. There was a spiritual connection between a clan member and a totem. Individuals communicated with their totem and received its protection. Pre-Columbians, as well as later Native Americans, believed that their animal totem protected them in the present, as well as in the afterlife.

Totems were passed down through the clan from generation to generation, and they often represented a clan's status, as well as its history. One way of displaying totems was by carving their features onto a cedar tree trunk. Totem poles were religious symbols, but they were also an expression of a clan's history and personality. The totems on a totem pole told the story of the clan, especially its adventures and accomplishments. To read a totem, one would start at the bottom and read upward.

Totem poles were displayed both inside and outside a dwelling. When they were posted outside, anyone passing by or entering the dwelling could tell which clan lived inside.

A totem

Everyone in the clan made a contribution to pre-Columbian society, even children. Without the modern conveniences we have today, the work was long and difficult, but working together helped to get it done.

HOW DID THEY MANAGE DAILY LIFE?

Chapter 3

Pre-Columbian people lived simple lives that centered on family and community. Every member of the clan, no matter how old or how young, was considered a valuable member of pre-Columbian society. Work was shared and tasks were done for the good of all. Day-to-day living mirrored a deep respect for the environment and for the people who shared it.

How Did they Organize Society?

Many pre-Columbian societies were governed by a chief, who was in charge of the clans. Only someone who could claim historical or mythical ancestors could be called a chief. These societies were hierarchical—the closer in relationship to a chief a person was, the more power he had. Usually a chief owned the home his clan lived in, and he and his family had the most private sections of the dwelling to themselves. Depending upon the culture, the natural resources surrounding a home might be owned by a particular chief, who claimed them for his specific clan, or they might be considered communal, and shared by many clans.

Many pre-Columbian societies had very distinct social classes consisting of nobles, commoners, and slaves. Commoners were free, but had no rights in a household. They had to pay tribute to the nobles, who belonged to the highest class. In the Mississippi culture, which settled near the Mississippi River around 800 CE, the very wealthy ate better food and lived in homes that were better protected from enemies. What made someone wealthy? Their land, jewelry, clothing, and other possessions (such as pottery).

Men and women from opposing tribes who were captured during war raids were forced into slavery. They had to perform the most difficult jobs, including chopping wood, hauling water, and tending fires. Slaves and non-slaves did not interact. Slaves were allowed to marry, but any children they had were also considered slaves.[1]

What Were Their Families Like?
Pre-Columbian family units usually consisted of a father, a mother, and many children. Families belonging to the same clan lived together in the same house. In many indigenous cultures, marriages were usually

Pre-Columbians lived in strong family units. Parents disciplined their children with love and kindness, and children were respectful of their elders.

arranged by the parents, and they were forbidden between clan members.[2] A man married only after he had proven himself as a hunter and warrior. His bride could be much older or much younger than he, but usually the couple were about the same age. An Algonquin man who wished to marry a woman gave her gifts like a tumpline, a log, and a kettle as symbols of their "engagement." In return, a woman gave her intended husband a bag of tobacco.[3]

One of the advantages of living in clans was that the workload of the community was shared. Every clan member had a job to do. The men hunted, fished, trapped and cleared the land for farming. They were also responsible for protecting the community and waging war.

The women cared for children, tended the fields and gardens in the farming community, butchered the meat, and foraged for food. They also cooked, sewed, erected the homes, and prepared the skins of the animals the men had trapped or hunted. Mothers often did all this work with a baby in a cradleboard strapped on her back.

The women of the Mississippi mound builder culture had an interesting way of keeping house. They swept broken pottery, the remnants

Women often skinned animals brought home by the men.

The fire built in the center of a pre-Columbian home was used both for cooking and for warmth. A room this size might house several members of a clan. It was a living and dining room by day and a bedroom by night.

of their meals, and other refuse outside their huts. Then they sprinkled a layer of fresh dirt over the pile. Thousands of years later, these piles yielded valuable troves of information about the daily life of this pre-Columbian society. Careful removal of the layers of dirt has revealed pieces of broken pottery, jewelry, feathers, and the bones of animals, among other things. Some animal bones contained spear points embedded in them. This information tells us what pre-Columbians ate, wore, and used. Who would have thought we would learn so much about early peoples from a pile of dirt?

Pre-Columbian parents regarded their children as treasured gifts—but that doesn't mean children could be lazy. Mothers taught their daughters how to cook, sew, and gather food, firewood, and water. Girls also learned basketry and pottery, and they helped the women of the clan look after the babies and very young children.

Boys were taught to hunt at around the age of ten. Sometimes they were sent into the forest and not allowed to return to their village until they had killed an animal. If a boy failed, the other tribe members looked down on him. If he was successful, a party was held in his honor. Boys also learned how to fish and fight like warriors. They took special "classes" in which they practiced fighting other boys in their clan.

Pre-Columbian children were raised by members of their extended families, and the use of physical punishment on children was rare. Children were taught to be obedient and respectful to their elders, nature, and their environment. Parents corrected their young ones in kindness, not anger.

Almost every family had a dog. People kept them as pets, and dogs helped haul and carry things.

What Was the Role of Women?
Pre-Columbian women may have shouldered a heavy workload, but they were also treated with great respect. In the Iroquois society, inheritance was matrilineal—that is, passed down through the mother's side of the family. In a matrilineal society, all property, including the longhouses, fields, and villages, belonged to the women, but the forests belonged to the men.[4]

Native American Indian dog

When he married, a man left his clan's dwelling and moved in with his wife and her relatives. Sons born into a matrilineal society were educated by their mother's brothers, not by their fathers. If a marriage didn't work out, the husband left his wife and returned to the clan of his mother, but his children continued to live with his wife and her clan. The oldest woman in a clan was the clan mother. She was considered the spiritual head of the clan. In some pre-Columbian cultures, a powerful clan mother might have more than one husband.

Clan mothers did not rule; however, they chose the male chief, guided him, and helped find a replacement for him when he died. The clan mothers oversaw the clan elders, who distributed the food and organized the planting and harvesting. The clan mothers also oversaw the planning of festivals and feasts.

Kivas

As pre-Columbian Pueblo civilizations became more sophisticated, so did their housing, and pit houses took on a new role. These round and rectangular structures were turned into kivas—underground rooms that had several functions. Men gathered in kivas to talk about matters that affected everyone in the community, such as when to plant and harvest crops, when to hold feasts, and the training of young boys.[5]

Kivas were also where the unmarried men and widowers lived. Women were forbidden from sleeping in a kiva, but they could bring their relatives food and other necessities. Some villages had separate kivas for women, but these were rare.

Kivas were also where religious ceremonies took place. Paintings of totems were on the walls. The participants, who were sworn to secrecy about what went on in the kiva, offered prayers and songs to the gods. What did they pray for? Mostly rain and a good harvest. When they prayed, they wore elaborate masks made of feathers and animal skins that depicted birds, sacred clowns, and various human forms. Part of the ceremony was public and took place in an aboveground plaza.

A kiva

What Part Did Religion Play?

Pre-Columbian peoples had various gods, but they all respected the god of creation, whom they referred to as the Great Spirit, or Master of Life. The early natives recognized spirituality in everything they did and believed that different spirits guided different activities. In the hunting cultures, prayers were offered to the spirits that guided the hunt, asking that the hunters be successful and return with enough meat to feed their families. Pre-Columbian Americans killed animals out of necessity: they needed to hunt for survival. At the same time, the hunters believed that the animals had their own spirits, and so they offered prayers to them, asking for their forgiveness for killing them. Some early peoples may have looked on animals as kin who were sacrificing their lives so that their brothers and sisters might be saved. They also believed that the flesh of an animal held all the traits of an animal, and a human that ate the animal received those traits.[6] Once an animal was killed, its body was treated with respect.

The Pueblo people prayed to the gods for a good harvest. They believed that spirits called kachinas (or katcinas) lived among the people

The sculpture Appeal to the Great Spirit, Boston

from the winter solstice until the summer solstice. These kachinas controlled rain, wind, and lightning. In special ceremonies honoring the kachinas, the men of the village dressed in various costumes to make themselves look like the gods. They also offered gifts of pottery and other items. Parents taught their children that the kachinas saw everything they did. To remind them to be on their best behavior, Pueblo parents gave their children kachina dolls to carry with them.

Both girls and boys were constantly searching for their spirit guides. To find them, young people would enter the forest alone and remain there without food until their spirit came to them in a vision. This religious ritual was called a vision quest, and it was a signal that a young person was ready for adulthood. Other religious rituals were conducted to gain the favor of friendly spirits and to appease the unfriendly ones.

Most pre-Columbian societies believed in an afterlife. The bodies of the dead were either cremated or buried in a curved position. Why curved? Curving, or flexing, the body took less burial space. Pre-Columbians believed that the afterlife was similar to earthly life. Pipes, jewelry, pottery, food, and weapons all went into a burial site. Sometimes a wife or slave was killed and buried along with the dead to accompany the spirit into the afterlife.

A pre-Columbian soul vessel. These burial vessels were used to hasten a person's soul into the afterlife.

Pre-Columbian Warriors

Boys trained to be warriors, but why did pre-Columbian peoples battle one another? They fought over living space and hunting and fishing rights. Often the leader of the tribe was also the military leader of the army, which was made up of the tribe's strongest and bravest men. Sometimes several groups of Native Americans would join together to fight against an attacking tribe that had large numbers of warriors.

Pre-Columbian Americans had an effective arsenal of weapons, including spears, knives, clubs, tomahawks, and bows and arrows. Most of these weapons were made of wood. The bows used for war were longer than those used for hunting. They could be as long as 6 feet (2 meters). Bowstring was made of twisted sinew, and arrowheads from flint, bone, or copper. A warrior carried 40 to 50 arrows in a leather or woven quiver. How far could an arrow fly? About 100 to 120 yards (30 to 35 meters). Pre-Columbian Americans also used a special club called a tomahawk to attack their enemies. Sometimes tomahawks were made from small trees. The top of the tomahawk was the tree's rootball, while the small trunk was its handle. Chipped stones were pressed into the rootball to inflict more injury.

Surprise was one tactic used by pre-Columbian warriors, and attacks usually came at dawn. Another strategy was to hide deep in the forest and ambush the enemy. "Uniforms" of leggings and vests made from brown deerskin camouflaged the warriors among the trees and other woodland plants.

After the arrival of Columbus, these pre-Columbian military strategies and weapons proved to be no match for the invading Europeans who fought with horses, guns, and cannons.

Pre-Columbian warriors from the Mississippi region

Clothing styles varied among the many types of pre-Columbian people, depending on how they made their living and where they lived. A particular headdress or hairstyle might also designate the leader of the clan or tribe.

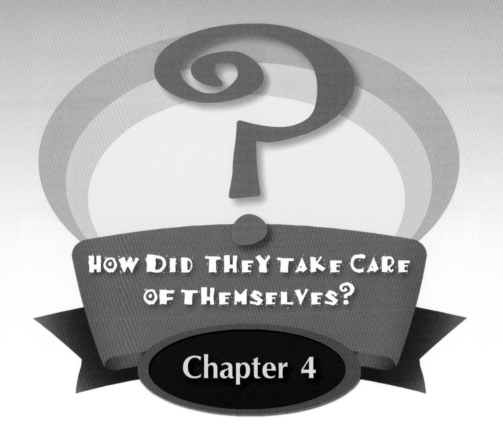

HOW DID THEY TAKE CARE OF THEMSELVES?

Chapter 4

Life for the pre-Columbian Americans was a daily fight for survival. Starvation, bad weather and wild animals threatened their well being daily. These early people learned to acclimate themselves to their environment. They used the resources that were available to them—animals, plants, water, and sunlight, and through trial and error, fashioned what they needed to make life more bearable.

What Did They Wear?

Early pre-Columbian peoples wore little or no clothing in the warmer months, just loincloths for the men and aprons for the women. Before they grew cotton, they made these garments from tough yucca fibers. How did they soften them to weave them? They chewed them. During the warm months, men and women either went barefoot or wore square-toed sandals made from yucca leaves, bark, or animal hides.

When the weather turned cold, the women wore knee-length skirts of either deerskin, elk skin, or buffalo fur that wrapped around the waist and fastened in the back. Men wore pants and vests made of fur, deerskin, yucca fibers, or animal skin lined with fur. They decorated the animal skins with feathers. Both men and women draped themselves in blankets made from fur or animal skins to keep warm. To get the animal skins soft enough to be used as clothing and blankets, they rubbed them with ashes or soaked them in a water-and-bark solution. Pre-Columbian Arctic dwellers often hunted in temperatures that were way below zero. They lined their caribou-skin parkas, pants, and boots with fur.[1] Snowshoes made from bark helped them walk on snow.

Later pre-Columbian cultures grew cotton, which was spun into yarn and woven into ponchos, shirts, and belts. Leather was wrapped around the legs and worn as a form of leggings to protect against thorns and brush, and to ward off snakebites. Post-Columbian invaders adapted the natives' use of these "leather stockings." One area of New York where pre-Columbian leather stockings were especially popular is known today as the Leather Stocking Region.[2] Clothing was decorated with feathers, embroidery, porcupine quills, and beads made from shells. Belts were made of twisted bark fiber, yarn, or braided human hair.

Until the age of four or five, children ran naked in the warm months, and wrapped themselves in blankets when it was cold.[3] After the age of five, they wore the same type of clothing as their parents.

Pre-Columbian Americans learned to make bracelets from naturally occurring copper, mica, silver, and gold. Both men and women wore rings, necklaces, and ear plugs made of shells, soft coal, colored stones, wood, bone, and seeds. Ear plugs were worn in the earlobe, which had to be stretched in order for the plug to fit. A particularly brave hunter might wear the claws or teeth of his prey on a cord around his neck.

Men wore a variety of hairstyles, depending on the culture. They parted their hair in the center and left it loose on either side, they braided it in a long ponytail in the back, or they shaved off a strip of

Leather stockings

hair from the forehead to the neck. Unmarried women styled their hair in elaborate ways. Married women usually cut their hair and used their locks as string, belts, or basket handles. Feathers and bones were worn as hair decorations by both men and women.

Many pre-Columbian cultures painted or tattooed their bodies. They did this not only for beauty; a warrior decorated his body as a way of asking for protection from his totem spirits.[4]

How Did They Treat Illness?

Pre-Columbian medicine treated the whole person—mind, body and spirit—regardless of which part of the body was hurt. How an illness was treated varied, depending on the culture as well as on the illness. Mostly, pre-Columbian people relied on three things to treat their illnesses: religion, natural plants, and magic.[5] The early Americans believed in a spirit world that was just as real as their earthly world. Each person and object on Earth had an identical spirit in the spirit world that guided and protected him or her. Early Native Americans believed that a person became ill when he or she fell out of balance with the environment, possessions, or the people with whom he or she lived. In some cases past deeds made a person ill. An opponent who cast a spell on a person could also make that person ill. In order to get well, the person had to resume a peaceful relationship with everything in his or her life, including the past.

Sassafras leaves. The roots were used to make tea.

A medicine man

Shamans, or medicine men, were healers who, by putting themselves in a trance, could go back and forth between Earth and the spirit world. The shamans of the Adena culture of the northeast woodlands wore deer antler headdresses. Either they were trained in healing, or they received their power to heal in a dream or from another healer or an ancestor. A checkup by a healer was a physical, mental, emotional, and spiritual exam. Depending upon the patient, a healer might prescribe prayer, meditation, ceremonies, or counseling to bring a person back into balance with his surroundings. The entire community came together to help heal a sick person. They chanted, sang, and danced around the sick person.

A shaman's "magic" could remove a spell. Often plant remedies were used as part of the healing process. The burning of sage or sweet grass during a healing ceremony could purify a person and lead to recovery. Boiled sage leaves applied to the skin relieved headaches and rheumatism. When the sage leaves were brewed into tea, they helped one recover from colds and the flu. Puffball fungus relieved swelling and sores, while rabbit brush stem and leaves were taken as cough medicine. Compresses made from passionflower helped relax strained muscles. Sassafras bark was chewed to clean teeth and prevent tooth decay. Purple coneflower was used to ease sore throats, toothaches, and headaches.

How Did They Make Everyday Objects?

Pre-Columbian peoples made most of their everyday items from stone, bone, or shell. In addition to spears and, later, arrows, many other objects were made from stone. Awls (pointed tools for making holes in wood or leather) were made from the bones of rabbits, deer, foxes, and birds. Knives were made from chert, a type of rock that contains graphite. The chert was carried from the quarries to the camps, where it was buried. Why was it buried? The stone was easier to work with if it was not exposed to air. Early peoples chipped, flaked, pounded, and hammered stone to make their knives and drills. Ax blades were carved from granite using a small boulder called a hammer stone. They were sharpened by scraping them against wet granite, then polished with pebbles, sand, and water.

Musical instruments like flutes and whistles were also made from the bones of animals. Antlers were made into clubs. The shoulder blades of elk, buffalo, or deer were used as shovels or scrapers. The horns of mountain sheep and goats were softened by boiling, then pressed into wooden molds, where they hardened and were later carved into tools, spoons, and other everyday objects. The ribs of other hunted animals were used in the framework for houses and boats, and as runners for sleds.

Clam and scallop shells were used as eating and drinking utensils. Conch shells were used as containers. Shells were also made into scrapers for cleaning animal skins, as well as knives, toys, dolls, amulets, beads, pendants, hairpins, combs, and tools used in weaving, netting, and sewing.[6] Bowls were made from soapstone.

Replica of a pre-Columbian skull-shaped whistle

American Indians continue to make the styles of pottery their ancestors did in the pre-Columbian days. Back then it was produced out of necessity. Today pre-Columbian-style pottery is considered art, and it is often used as decoration.

HOW DID THEY SPEND THEIR LEISURE TIME?

Chapter 5

Once pre-Columbian cultures started to depend on agriculture for food, people had the time and energy to devote to other activities. More care and attention could be given to the making of baskets and pottery. Producing these items became less work and more fun.

Basketry and Pottery

In later pre-Columbian years, women began making baskets and pottery. For baskets, they used just about anything that would bend, including roots, reeds, willow branches, grass, bark, ferns, hemp, yucca fibers, and even human hair. Baskets were often decorated with beads, porcupine quills, and feathers. They were used to gather and store food, carry babies, and transport items. When coated with pitch or mud, baskets were used as pots for cooking.

Pre-Columbian people began making pottery around 500–700 CE. Early pottery was created by coating the inside of a basket with mud and leaving it to dry in the sun. Later pottery was made stronger by adding crushed rock and sand to the mud, shaping pieces by hand, and then firing them (exposing them to high temperatures). Early pottery was gray or black-gray, but later pottery was painted with red ocher. Jars, pitchers, bottles, pots, cups, dippers and bowls, and gourds were some of the useful objects pre-Columbians learned to make from pottery. Pottery and baskets were useful items, but making them provided a creative outlet as well. Pottery, especially, developed into an art form. Some pieces of pre-Columbian pottery survive today.

What Games Did They Play?

Pre-Columbian people worked hard, but they also found time for fun and relaxation. Games weren't just for kids; all members of pre-Columbian society participated in fun activities. The competition taught young people morals, physical fitness, and social skills.[1] Games also taught children the skills they could use as adults. Relay races taught young men how to be swift on their feet, a skill needed to successfully hunt deer. Good running skills could also help a young person earn a place as a messenger—a person who ran back and forth between camps.

Young children played their own games. One was similar to catch, only they used stones instead of balls. The pre-Columbian version of marbles was played with small, round pebbles. Dice were made from animal teeth or the bones of small animals. The games with dice were simple. Each player threw the dice, and the person who came up with the highest number won the game. In another game, a target number was agreed upon. All players threw the dice, and the one who reached the target number, or came closest to it, was the winner.

Pre-Columbian people also enjoyed simple guessing games. In one such game, a player hid a marked stick in one of his hands. His opponent had to guess which hand it was in. In another guessing game, a small object was hidden and

*Pueblo Indian
girl playing*

the players had to guess where it was. When playing the hand game, the players often brought in singers and dancers to distract their opponents. One song that pre-Columbians sang when playing the hand game went like this:

Now I go to seek my horses!
So here I stand and look about me!
So here I stand and look about me!
Now I go to seek my horses![2]

Men played Chungke (sometimes referred to as "chunkey stone"), a game played with a stone disk and a long forked pole. Two people played this game. One player rolled the disk, and then both players would charge after it. The object was to get your pole through the hole of the rolling disk. Whichever player did this was the winner.

Pre-Columbian people worked hard but they also made time for play. Games like Chungke were used to build endurance and strength for hunting and other survival activities.

People who lived in nearby towns often competed against one another in the game of Chungke. In addition to fun and relaxation, games were used by pre-Columbians to settle differences and resolve conflicts. Even these early people knew it was better to solve disputes using a game instead of war.

How Did They Celebrate Special Events?

For most pre-Columbian societies, summer was the time for celebrating with feasts and ceremonies. Every life stage was considered worthy of a feast, including births, first hunts, and marriages. Most celebrations included dancing.

Pre-Columbian Plains peoples also took part in religious feasts that were held to honor the spirits. One common religious celebration was the Sun Dance, for which a warrior endured the physical discomfort of fasting for four days while dancing almost continuously. He offered up his physical discomfort to the spirits, and in exchange, he asked for their spiritual protection when he went to war.

The Iroquois held a Maple Ceremony celebrating the sap that flowed from the maple trees each spring, and a Green Corn Ceremony in which they gave thanks for the corn crop. Midwinter was a holiday that concluded the old year and welcomed the new one. This holiday asked the gods for many blessings for the new year. It was six days of celebrations, which included feasting, dancing, and playing games.[3]

The northern hunters celebrated their community with songs and dances. They danced in circles to demonstrate that people who lived together shared both the good and bad of a common world. Dancing also celebrated their connection to the spirit world.[4]

A Vanishing Way of Life

Columbus was only the first of many European explorers who set out to conquer the New World and claim it for their leaders. Over the first hundred years after Columbus's discovery, Europeans who explored North America found communities of pre-Columbian people that were organized, productive, and self-sufficient. These native peoples were for the most part peaceful, and lived with a deep respect for nature and all living things. Their way of life faded a little more with each wave of European exploration.

Christopher Columbus

Many explorers were cruel and heartless and did not recognize the right of pre-Columbian peoples to live on lands that had been theirs for hundreds of thousands of years. Some European explorers did not even see these natives as human beings, and considered them instead as savages to be exploited and enslaved. Huge numbers of pre-Columbian peoples died at the hands of ruthless conquerors, such as Hernando De Soto and Francisco Vásquez de Coronado. Those natives who were not cruelly exploited were still not safe from the Europeans. Diseases brought over from Europe, for which the pre-Columbians had no resistance, killed millions of native people. So did guns and alcohol—two things pre-Columbians had never seen before their encounters with the "White Man." Over time, Native Americans became subject to the "White Man's" laws. One example of this is the Trail of Tears—when Native Americans were forcibly removed from their homelands to reservations in 1831. Many died of exposure, starvation, and disease. Another example of the ill-treatment of native peoples occurred at Wounded Knee Creek in South Dakota. More than 150 Native Americans were massacred in 1890 as the U.S. Cavalry attempted to relocate them to Nebraska.

What we know today about pre-Columbian peoples comes from archaeological artifacts and other discoveries. A few Native American communities scattered across the United States continue to practice some of the customs handed down from their ancient ancestors, but for the most part, the pre-Columbian lifestyle has all but disappeared.

MAKE A DREAM CATCHER

Early as well as later Native Americans hung dream catchers above their sleeping quarters. They believed that the bad dreams were caught by the netting and beads, while the good dreams passed through and into the mind of the one who slept.

To make a dream catcher, you will need the following supplies. Most are available at craft stores, but you might be able to find a few feathers right in your own backyard.

Long chenille stems
About 3 feet of twine, yarn, or string
Colorful beads
Feathers

Instructions:

1. Bend the chenille stems into a circle.
2. Tie one end of the twine anywhere on the chenille stem circle.
3. String three beads onto the twine, pushing the beads to the end by the chenille stems.
4. Wrap the twine around the opposite end of the chenille stem loop.
5. Continue stringing beads and wrapping the twine until you have made a web design within the circle of the loop.
6. Tie three pieces of twine to the bottom of the loop so that they hang off the loop.
7. Tie a few beads and the feathers to these hanging strings.
8. Hang your dream catcher above your bed. Sweet dreams!

BCE

c. 12,000–10,000
The first Pre-Columbian Americans walk from Siberia and settle in North America; Clovis points are developed

c. 10,000–7000
Ice age ends; Bering Land Bridge is flooded and nomadic migration ends

9000–6000
Big game hunters pursued mammoth and bison in the Plains

8500
The atlatl is first used

7000
North American climate change causes large mammals to become extinct and forests and grasslands to be created

5500
Food grinding tools are first used

5000
Wild corn appears; Northeast big game hunters begin hunting smaller animals; Foraged foods begin to be stored for lean times

3000
The wild horse that greeted early pre-Columbians becomes extinct

2000
Copper is mined and worked in the Great Lakes region; Corn is a well-established crop for Middle Americans; Above-ground dwellings replace pit houses in Central America

1500
Pre-Columbians living in southeast North America produce pottery

1000–700
Evidence of the beginning of the Woodland culture. It lasts until about the time of European contact

750
Mississippi culture builds large temple mounds

CE

400

Settlement of Anasazi in Four Corners (Arizona, Colorado, Utah, New Mexico) of the United States

500

The bow and arrow begins to be used for hunting and warfare

500–900

Agriculture first appears among pre-Columbian peoples

985–1000

The Norsemen discover Greenland and Vineland

1000–1300

Anasazi build cliff homes

1492

Christopher Columbus discovers the New World

1691

Native Americans introduce the feast of Thanksgiving to English colonists

A modern group reenacts the ancient tradition of a pow-wow.

Introduction: Unami Passes His Test

1. Clarissa Confer, *Daily Life in Pre-Columbian Native America* (Westport, Connecticut: Greenwood Press, 2008), p. 174.

Chapter 1: How Did They Get Their Food?

1. Jesse D. Jennings, ed., *Ancient Native Americans* (San Francisco: W.H. Freeman and Company, 1978), p.23.
2. Jonathan Norton Leonard, *Ancient America* (New York: Time-Life Books, 1967), p. 17.
3. James M. Volo and Dorothy Denneen Volo, *Family Life in Native America* (Westport, Connecticut: Greenwood Press, 2007), p. 133.
4. Charles C. Mann, *1491: New Revelations of the Americas Before Columbus* (New York: Alfred A. Knopf, 2005), p. 81.
5. Ibid., p. 82.

Chapter 2: How Did They Build Their Homes?

1. James M. Volo and Dorothy Denneen Volo, *Family Life in Native America* (Westport, Connecticut: Greenwood Press, 2006), p. 82.
2. Stacy Kowtko, *Nature and the Environment in Pre-Columbian American Life* (Westport, Connecticut: Greenwood Press, 2007), p. 82.
3. Clarissa Confer. *Daily Life in Pre-Columbian Native America* (Westport, Connecticut: Greenwood Press, 2008), p. 65.
4. Paul S. Martin, George I. Quimby, and Donald Colier, *Indians Before Columbus: Twenty Thousand Years of North American History Revealed by Archaeology* (Chicago: The University of Chicago Press, 1947), p. 101.

Chapter 3: How Did They Manage Daily Life?

1. Clarissa Confer, *Daily Life in Pre-Columbian Native America* (Westport, Connecticut: Greenwood Press, 2008), p. 159.
2. James M. Volo and Dorothy Denneen Volo, *Family Life in Native America* (Westport, Connecticut: Greenwood Press, 2007), p. 45.
3. Ibid., p. 78.
4. Karen Olsen Bruhns and Karen E. Stothert, *Women in Ancient America* (Norman: University of Oklahoma Press, 1999), 123.
5. Alvin M. Josephy, Jr., *America in 1492: The World of the Indian Peoples Before the Arrival of Columbus* (New York: Alfred A. Knopf, 1993), pp.109–110.
6. Volo and Volo, p. 145.

Chapter 4: How Did They Take Care of Themselves?

1. Charles C. Mann, *1491: New Revelations of the Americas Before Columbus* (New York: Alfred A. Knopf, 2005), p. 40.
2. James M. Volo and Dorothy Denneen Volo, *Family Life in Native America* (Westport, Connecticut: Greenwood Press, 2007), p.120.
3. Ibid., 119.
4. Mann, p.202.
5. Stacy Kowtko, *Nature and the Environment in Pre-Columbian American Life* (Westport, Connecticut: Greenwood Press, 2007), p. 121.
6. Paul S. Martin, George I. Quimby, and Donald Colier, *Indians Before Columbus: Twenty Thousand Years of North American History Revealed by Archaeology* (Chicago: The University of Chicago Press, 1947), p. 47.

Chapter 5: How Did They Spend Their Leisure Time?

1. Stacy Kowtko, *Nature and the Environment in Pre-Columbian American Life* (Westport, Connecticut: Greenwood Press, 2007), p. 156.
2. Stewart Culin, *Games of North American Indians: Volume 2–Games of Chance* (Lincoln: University of Nebraska Press, 1992), p. 286.
3. Clarissa Confer, *Daily Life in Pre-Columbian Native America* (Westport, Connecticut: Greenwood Press, 2008), p. 20.
4. Alvin M. Josephy, Jr., *America in 1492: The World of the Indian Peoples Before the Arrival of Columbus* (New York: Alfred A. Knopf, 1993), p. 36.

FURTHER READING

Books

Freedman, Russell. *Who Was First? Discovering the Americas.* Broomall, Penn.: Clarion, 2007.

Lacey, Minna. *Christopher Columbus.* London: Usborne, 2005.

Macfarlan, Allan A. *Native American Tales and Legends.* Mineola, N.Y.: Dover Publications, 2001.

Williams, Colleen. *Native American Family Life.* Broomall, Penn.: Mason Crest Publishers, 2002.

Wingate, Philippa, and Struan Reid. *Who Were the First North Americans?* Tulsa: E.D.C. Publishing, 2003.

Works Consulted

Berzok, Linda Murray. *American Indian Food.* Westport, Connecticut: Greenwood Press, 2005.

Bruhns, Karen Olsen, and Karen E. Stothert. *Women in Ancient America.* Norman: University of Oklahoma Press, 1999.

Confer, Clarissa. *Daily Life in Pre-Columbian Native America.* Westport, Connecticut: Greenwood Press, 2008.

Culin, Stewart. *Games of North American Indians: Volume 2–Games of Chance.* Lincoln: University of Nebraska Press, 1992.

Deneven, William M., ed. *The Native Population of the Americas in 1492* (2nd Ed.) Madison: University of Wisconsin Press, 1992.

Fagan, Brian M. *Kingdoms of Gold, Kingdoms of Jade: The Americas Before Columbus.* New York: Thames and Hudson, 1991.

Huyghe, Patrick. *Columbus Was Last: From 200,000 B.C. to 1492, A Heretical History of Who Was First.* New York: Hyperion, 1992.

Jennings, Jesse D., ed. *Ancient Native Americans.* San Francisco: W.H. Freeman and Company, 1978.

Johansen, Bruce E. *The Native Peoples of North America: A History Volumes I and II.* Westport, Connecticut: Praeger, 2007.

Johnson, Michael G., and Richard Hook. *Encyclopedia of Native Tribes of North America.* Buffalo, New York: Firefly Books, 2007.

Josephy, Alvin M., Jr. *America in 1492: The World of the Indian Peoples Before the Arrival of Columbus.* New York: Alfred A. Knopf, 1993.

Kowtko, Stacy. *Nature and the Environment in Pre-Columbian American Life.* Westport, Connecticut: Greenwood Press, 2007.

Leonard, Jonathan Norton. *Ancient America.* New York: Time-Life Books, 1967.

Mann, Charles C. *1491: New Revelations of the Americas Before Columbus.* New York: Alfred A. Knopf, 2005.

Martin, Paul S., George I. Quimby, and Donald Colier. *Indians Before Columbus: Twenty Thousand Years of North American History Revealed by Archaeology.* Chicago: The University of Chicago Press, 1947.

Thomas, David Hurst, Jay Miller, Richard White Peter Nabokov, Philip J. Deloria. *The Native Americans: An Illustrated History.* Atlanta: Turner Publishing, Inc. 1993.

Volo, James M., and Dorothy Denneen Volo. *Family Life in Native America.* Westport, Connecticut: Greenwood Press, 2007.

On the Internet

Ancient Canada: The Inuit and Native Cultures of Canada
http://www.theancientweb.com/explore/content.aspx?content_id=6

Fruitlands Museum: Native American Collection, The Dugout Canoe Project
http://www.fruitlands.org/indian

Native American Homes: "Wigwams, Longhouses, Tepees, Lodges and Other American Indian Houses"
http://www.native-languages.org/houses.htm

Ojibway Indian Fact Sheet: Facts for Kids
http://www.bigorrin.org/chippewa_kids.htm

U.S. Department of the Interior, National Park Service: "Bering Land Bridge National Preserve"
http://www.nps.gov/bela/historyculture/index.htm